A Miracle for Awa

by Ellie Grace Cole

Based on a true story.

A Miracle for Awa

© 2024 by Ellie Grace Cole

Published by Bolígrafo Books

An imprint of Grafo House Publishing

Tulsa, OK | Guadalajara, Mexico

ISBN   978-1-963127-18-8 (hardbound)

978-1-963127-19-5 (paperback)

978-1-963127-20-1 (eBook)

Printed in the United States of America

27 26 25 24   1 2 3 4

Bonjour! My name is Ellie, and I live in Mali, Africa, with my mom, dad, goofy little brother, sweet little sister, dog, cat, and seven bunnies. We are here to help people discover how much God loves and cares for them.

When I was ten years old, I saw God answer our prayers for some new friends. This is the story of that amazing miracle.

It was a hot, hot day in Mali, Africa, and our air conditioning had stopped working. My parents hired two men named Idrissa and Malik to come and fix it. They were very kind.

After talking with them for a little while, my parents discovered that Idrissa and Malik were "people of peace." They were people who wanted to know the truth about Jesus.

The next week, Idrissa invited my family and Malik to go over to his house. When we got there, we met Awa, Idrissa's wife. We talked, ate yummy Mali food, talked some more, and ate more delicious food.

My little brother, sister, and I climbed the mango trees and watched
all the pigeons, turkeys, chickens, guineas, dogs, and children wander
around below, stirring up the dust.

When my family started to share the Bible with Idrissa, Awa, and Malik, they were very interested, and they wanted to know more. We were so excited!

After that, we started meeting with our new friends each week to discover truth from the Bible together. We call this a "Discovery Bible Study."

One day my family and I were at Idrissa and Awa's house, and Malik was there too. While we were sitting under the mango tree, my dad asked them a question that is used in a Discovery Bible Study. "What is a challenge you or your family have been facing lately?"

Awa looked at the ground and sighed. "Well," she started, "do you see that water hose by the front door?"

My mom, dad, brother, sister, and I all looked. We saw a short, brown water hose that looked very broken. "Yes," we answered, wondering what she would say next.

Then Awa explained, "That is where we used to get water to fill up all ten of our green jugs. Our large family uses these ten jugs of water every day for all of our cooking, cleaning, and bathing. But the water faucet hasn't worked in many, many years. Nothing comes out. I have to wake up super early while my family sleeps, load the ten empty water jugs in my broken, heavy, wooden wheelbarrow, and carry them down the steep hill to the market."

"In the market, there is a big water faucet where all the women fill up their water jugs. I have to stand in line for three long, tiring hours while all of the women in front of me fill up their jugs. When I finally get to the front of the line, I fill up my ten jugs. But then, I have to put the heavy jugs back into the wheelbarrow and push with all of my might to get back up the very steep hill to my home. I am so tired and I don't know how much longer I can do it!"

Immediately, my family and I wondered if there was anything we could do to help our new friends. After asking a lot of questions and thinking as hard as we could, we realized there was nothing we could do—but pray!

We told them, "We will pray in the name of Jesus and ask God to give you water."

A few weeks later, we were driving to Idrissa and Awa's house to study the Bible with them and Malik. When we were almost there, my dad said, "Oh, wait! We are only five minutes away and we forgot to pray!"

Every time our family traveled to Idrissa and Awa's house, we would pray for them in Jesus' name. So for the last five minutes of the trip, we all prayed for the water to come to their house. We didn't stop praying until we got there.

When we opened the front door to go into the house,
we suddenly heard squealing. Worried, we rushed inside.
"What's wrong!?" we asked.

"The water!" Awa yelled. "The water just started working
five minutes ago!" She pointed toward the broken, brown water hose.
It was now gushing out water.

My dad turned to my siblings and me with a big smile on his face. "Jesus answered our prayers! The water started working right when we were praying in the car!"

The water poured out of the brown water hose until the last jug was full, all the way to the top. Then the water stopped.

I had an amazing feeling of thankfulness and joy that filled my heart to the brim—just like all ten of Awa's water jugs. We all danced, laughed, and worshiped God for the amazing miracle he had done.

In Mali, April is the hottest, driest month. But right after the water filled the last jug, it started to rain.

"But it never rains in April!" I said. "It must be from God!"

I imagined that the rain was a wink from Jesus, like He was saying, "You're welcome." Hearing from Jesus is one of the best things in the world for me!

When we visited a week later,
we all rushed inside their house and asked,
"Is the water still running?!"

Awa looked at us with a big smile on her face and
tears in her eyes and said, "Yes! The water gives us
all we need for the day, and then it stops. It has
only come to our house, up here on the hill."

She told us that every morning, water started
pouring from the brown water hose. And every
morning, as soon as all ten of her water jugs were
filled to the cap, the water would stop. She was
seeing God's miracle again and again.

Awa and her family needed a miracle very badly, and God helped them. When we prayed for our friends, God heard us, and He answered.

My family and I couldn't have been happier. I felt so grateful that God answered our prayers! We praised God and worshiped Him and never wanted to stop.

That day at Awa's house, I learned that God can do extraordinary things!

"God can do anything, you know—far more than you could ever imagine or guess or request in your wildest dreams!" Ephesians 3:20 MSG

Ellie lives in West Africa with her parents, two siblings, two dogs and a cat. She began writing **A Miracle for Awa** at the age of eleven after experiencing a miracle first hand in Bamako, Mali. Growing up on the mission field, Ellie has developed a deep passion for helping others encounter God through Discovery Bible Studies. Her admiration of the love and power of God shines through writing.

In addition to writing, she enjoys basketball, laughing with her friends and playing with her dog, Jada. This book marks her debut as an author, and she is already planning her next story, excited to inspire and captivate young readers.

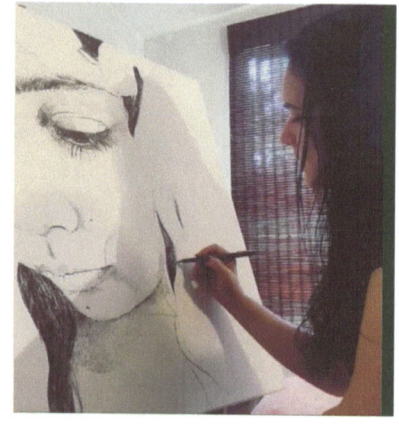

Olivia Fregoso is an illustrator and fine arts painter who has worked with clients from around the world for over two decades. Her extensive experience includes graphic design for newspapers and magazines in Mexico and Latin America, commissioned art pieces, custom design work, and book design, including several high-profile books that have been presented at the prestigious Feria Internacional de Libros (International Book Fair) in Guadalajara. She is currently building her company **Olivia Fregoso ART / ILU.** She has taught illustration and painting workshops for twelve years. She has exhibited her art in Mexico, London and France.

Follow Olivia online at
www.instagram/oliviafregosoart
www.behance.net/oliviafregosomedrano

How To Have a Discovery Bible Study

You can do a Discovery Bible Study, too!
Just grab a Bible and some friends
and walk through these questions together.

What are you thankful for?
What is a challenge in your life today?

Next, read a passage from the Bible at least two times.
Then, have someone retell the story in their own words.
After retelling, answer these next four questions:

What does this story tell us about God?
What does this story tell us about people?
How can we obey the passage this week?
Who can you tell the story to this week?

For more information about making disciples
or Discovery Bible Studies, you can go to
www.finalcommand.com

Awa filling her water jugs.